*Complicated* Kris Northern

"This image illustrates some of the best qualities of fractals—infinity, reiteration, and self similarity."– **Kris Northern**

# Investigations

### IN NUMBER, DATA, AND SPACE®

**Editorial offices:** Glenview, Illinois • Parsippany, New Jersey • New York, New York
**Sales offices:** Boston, Massachusetts • Duluth, Georgia
Glenview, Illinois • Coppell, Texas • Sacramento, California • Mesa, Arizona

The Investigations curriculum was developed by TERC, Cambridge, MA.

This material is based on work supported by the National Science Foundation ("NSF") under Grant No.ESI-0095450. Any opinions, findings, and conclusions or recommendations expressed in this material are those of the author(s) and do not necessarily reflect the views of the National Science Foundation.

ISBN: 0-328-24040-0

ISBN: 978-0-328-24040-1

13 14 15 16 17-V031-16 15 14 13 12 11

# Partners, Teams, and Paper Clips

## Investigation 4

# Problems About Two Groups (page 1 of 2)

Solve the problems. Show your work.

1. 12 children from Room A want to play kickball.
   10 children from Room B also want
   to play. Can they make 2 equal teams?

   How many people would be on each team? _____

2. Ms. Todd's class is going to play a game in
   pairs. There are 12 boys and 10 girls. Can
   everyone have a partner?

   How many pairs would there be? _____

3. There are 12 girls and 11 boys in Mr. Fox's class.
   Can everyone have a partner?

   How many pairs would there be? _____

# Problems About Two Groups (page 2 of 2)

Solve the problems. Show your work.

**4.** 16 children from Room A want to play soccer.
11 children from Room B also want to play.
Can they make 2 equal teams?

How many people would be on each team? _____

**5.** At recess 17 girls want to play baseball. 13 boys
want to play, too. Can they make 2 equal teams?

How many people would be on each team? _____

**6.** Ms. Ortega's class has 15 girls and 15 boys.
Can everyone have a partner?

How many pairs would there be? _____

# At the Amusement Park

Solve each problem. Show your work.

**NOTE** Students determine which numbers can and cannot make equal groups of 2 or 2 equal teams.

**SMH** 41–42

**1.** 6 girls and 7 boys want to ride the Python roller coaster together. Can everyone have a partner to ride with?

How many pairs would there be? _____

**2.** Two groups can go into the Haunted House at one time. There are 26 children in line. Can they make two equal groups?

How many people would be in each group? _____

## Ongoing Review

**3.** David has 13 pets. Some of them are mice, and some of them are hamsters. How many of David's 13 pets could be mice?

Which answer could **not** be correct?

(A) 12          (B) 11          (C) 1          (D) 0

# Missing Numbers

Write the missing numbers
on the counting strips.

**NOTE** Students practice skip counting
by groups of 2s, 5s, and 10s.

SMH 37, 38, 39

| | | |
|---|---|---|
| 112 | | 160 |
| 114 | | |
| | 125 | 140 |
| | | 130 |
| | | |
| | | |
| 122 | 140 | |
| 124 | 145 | |
| | | 90 |

# Partners and Teams (page 1 of 2)

Solve each problem. Show your work.

**NOTE** Students think about numbers that can and cannot make groups of 2 or 2 equal teams.

SMH 41–42

**1.** Mrs. Abel's class has 10 boys and 9 girls. Can everyone have a partner?

How many pairs would there be? _____

**2.** 11 girls want to play kickball. 7 boys also want to play. Can they make 2 equal teams?

How many people would be on each team? _____

# Partners and Teams (page 2 of 2)

Solve each problem. Show your work.

**3.** Mr. Yoshi has 9 girls and 7 boys in his class.
Can everyone have a partner?

How many pairs would there be? _____

**4.** There are 8 boys and 11 girls who want to play
soccer. Can they make 2 equal teams?

How many people would be on each team? _____

# Can You Make . . . ? (page 1 of 2) ✏️WRITING

Today's Number is <u>24</u>.

**1.** Is 24 even or odd? _____

**2.** Can you make 24 with two EVEN numbers?

_____ + _____ = 24          _____ + _____ = 24

If you think you cannot, explain why:

_____

_____

**3.** Can you make 24 with two ODD numbers?

_____ + _____ = 24          _____ + _____ = 24

If you think you cannot, explain why:

_____

_____

**4.** Can you make 24 with an EVEN and an ODD number?

_____ + _____ = 24          _____ + _____ = 24

If you think you cannot, explain why:

_____

_____

# Can You Make . . . ? (page 2 of 2)

Today's Number is 23.

**5.** Is 23 even or odd? _____

**6.** Can you make 23 with two EVEN numbers?

_____ + _____ = 23      _____ + _____ = 23

If you think you cannot, explain why:

_____

_____

**7.** Can you make 23 with two ODD numbers?

_____ + _____ = 23      _____ + _____ = 23

If you think you cannot, explain why:

_____

_____

**8.** Can you make 23 with an EVEN and an ODD number?

_____ + _____ = 23      _____ + _____ = 23

If you think you cannot, explain why:

_____

_____

# What Happens When . . . ? (page 1 of 3)

What happens when you add
two ODD numbers together?

**1.** Try these:

9 + 9 = _____      Is the answer even or odd? _____

11 + 7 = _____      Is the answer even or odd? _____

15 + 23 = _____      Is the answer even or odd? _____

**2.** Now try some of your own:

_____ + _____ = _____      Is the answer even or odd? _____

_____ + _____ = _____      Is the answer even or odd? _____

_____ + _____ = _____      Is the answer even or odd? _____

**3.** What do you get when you add two ODD numbers together?

_____

**4.** Do you think this is **always** true? _____

**5.** Why do you think so? _____

_____

_____

**Partners, Teams, and Paper Clips**

# What Happens When . . . ? (page 2 of 3)

What happens when you add
two EVEN numbers together?

6. Try these:

8 + 8 = _____     Is the answer even or odd? _____

12 + 6 = _____     Is the answer even or odd? _____

14 + 20 = _____     Is the answer even or odd? _____

7. Now try some of your own:

____ + ____ = ____ Is the answer even or odd? _____

____ + ____ = ____ Is the answer even or odd? _____

____ + ____ = ____ Is the answer even or odd? _____

8. What do you get when you add two EVEN numbers together?

_____

9. Do you think this is **always** true? _____

10. Why do you think so? _____

_____

_____

# What Happens When . . . ? (page 3 of 3)

What happens when you add an EVEN
number and an ODD number?

**11.** Try these:

$8 + 7 =$ _____ Is the answer even or odd? _____

$11 + 6 =$ _____ Is the answer even or odd? _____

$14 + 23 =$ _____ Is the answer even or odd? _____

**12.** Now try some of your own:

_____ + _____ = _____ Is the answer even or odd? _____

_____ + _____ = _____ Is the answer even or odd? _____

_____ + _____ = _____ Is the answer even or odd? _____

**13.** What do you get when you add an EVEN
number and an ODD number?

_____

**14.** Do you think this is **always** true? _____

**15.** Why do you think so? _____

_____

_____

**Partners, Teams, and Paper Clips**                    **Daily Practice**

# Telling Time

Read each clock. Record what time it is. Record and draw what time it will be in 1 hour. Write the time in words.

**NOTE** Students practice telling, recording, and determining what time it will be to the quarter hour.

**SMH** 137–138, 140, 141

| What time is it now? | What time will it be in one hour? |
|---|---|
| ⏰    :    nine fifteen | ⏰    : |
| ⏰    : | ⏰    : |
| ⏰    : | ⏰    : |
| ⏰    : | ⏰    : |
| ⏰    : | ⏰    : |

# Adding Even and Odd Numbers (page 1 of 2)

> **NOTE** Students investigate what happens when you add two even numbers or two odd numbers.
>
> **SMH** 41–42

Solve each problem. Circle EVEN or ODD for each answer.

**1.** 6 + 8 = _____      EVEN      ODD

**2.** 12 + 4 = _____      EVEN      ODD

**3.** 16 + 20 = _____      EVEN      ODD

Answer each question. Explain your thinking.

**4.** What happens when you add two even numbers?

_____

_____

_____

**5.** Is this true for **any** two even numbers?

**6.** Explain (or show) **why** this is true.

# Adding Even and Odd Numbers (page 2 of 2) ✏️WRITING

Solve each problem. Circle EVEN or ODD for each answer.

**7.** 7 + 9 = _____          EVEN          ODD

**8.** 13 + 5 = _____          EVEN          ODD

**9.** 15 + 21 = _____          EVEN          ODD

Answer each question. Explain your thinking.

**10.** What happens when you add two odd numbers?

_____

_____

_____

**11.** Is this true for **any** two odd numbers?

**12.** Explain (or show) **why** this is true.

# Even or Odd?

Will the sum be even or odd?
Circle one word.
Solve the problem to check
your answer.

**NOTE** Students use what they know about adding even and odd numbers to determine whether sums will be even or odd. They also practice addition combinations.

**SMH** 41–42

|  | Will the sum be even or odd? | What is the sum? |
|---|---|---|
| **1.** 2 + 4 | EVEN    ODD |  |
| **2.** 6 + 3 | EVEN    ODD |  |
| **3.** 8 + 7 | EVEN    ODD |  |
| **4.** 9 + 2 | EVEN    ODD |  |
| **5.** 6 + 6 | EVEN    ODD |  |

# Ongoing Review

**6.** How many boats are there?

(A) 19

(B) 20

(C) 21

(D) 22

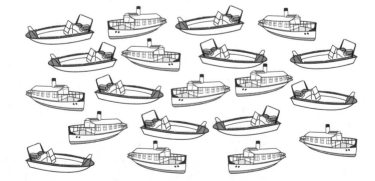

# How Much Money?

How much money does each student have? How much more does each one need to make $1.00?

**NOTE** Students practice counting money and determining the difference between an amount and $1.00.

**SMH** 19, 20, 21

---

**1.**

Kira has _____.

She needs _____ to make $1.00.

**2.**

Franco has _____.

He needs _____ to make $1.00.

**3.**

Jake has _____.

He needs _____ to make $1.00.

**4.**

Sally has _____.

She needs _____ to make $1.00.

---

# Plus 9 or 10 BINGO Gameboard

> **NOTE** This game offers practice with plus 9 and plus 10 addition combinations.
>
> **SMH** 51, 52, G11

| | | | | | |
|---|---|---|---|---|---|
| **9** | **10** | **11** | **12** | **13** | **14** |
| **15** | **16** | **17** | **18** | **19** | **20** |
| **20** | **19** | **18** | **17** | **16** | **15** |
| **14** | **13** | **12** | **11** | **10** | **9** |
| **9** | **10** | **11** | **12** | **13** | **14** |
| **15** | **16** | **17** | **18** | **19** | **20** |

# Subtracting Tens

Solve these problems. Fill in the answers on the 100 chart below.

**NOTE** Students practice subtracting 10 and multiples of 10 and sequencing numbers 1–100.

**SMH** 24

**1.** 43 − 10 = ____   **2.** 54 − 20 = ____   **3.** 95 − 50 = ____

**4.** 37 − 20 = ____   **5.** 67 − 30 = ____   **6.** 49 − 20 = ____

**7.** 22 − 10 = ____   **8.** 86 − 30 = ____   **9.** 64 − 40 = ____

**10.** Fill in the other missing numbers on the 100 chart.

|    |    | 3  |    |    | 6  |    |    |    | 10 |
|----|----|----|----|----|----|----|----|----|----|
|    |    |    | 15 |    |    |    |    | 19 |    |
| 21 |    |    | 25 | 26 |    |    |    |    |    |
|    | 33 |    |    | 36 |    | 38 |    |    |    |
|    | 42 |    | 44 |    |    |    |    | 49 | 50 |
|    | 52 |    |    | 55 |    | 57 |    |    |    |
|    |    | 64 |    |    |    | 68 |    |    |    |
| 71 |    |    | 75 |    | 77 |    |    |    | 80 |
|    | 83 |    |    | 86 |    |    | 89 |    |    |
| 91 |    |    |    | 96 |    |    |    |    |    |

20

# The Remaining Combinations (page 1 of 2)

Choose 3 pairs of problems that are hard for you to remember.

**NOTE** Students are finding ways to remember facts that are hard for them. Ask your child to explain how the clues help.

 **SMH** 53

| 3 + 5<br>5 + 3 | 4 + 7<br>7 + 4 | 3 + 8<br>8 + 3 | 5 + 8<br>8 + 5 |
|---|---|---|---|
| 3 + 6<br>6 + 3 | 5 + 7<br>7 + 5 | 4 + 8<br>8 + 4 | 6 + 8<br>8 + 6 |

1. _____ is hard for me to remember.

   Here is a clue that can help me:

2. _____ is hard for me to remember.

   Here is a clue that can help me:

3. _____ is hard for me to remember.

   Here is a clue that can help me:

# The Remaining Combinations (page 2 of 2)

Now solve these combinations.

**4.** $3 + 5 =$ _____   **5.** $7 + 4 =$ _____

**6.** $6 + 8 =$ _____   **7.** $8 + 3 =$ _____

**8.** $3 + 6 =$ _____   **9.** $8 + 5 =$ _____

**10.** $7 + 5 =$ _____   **11.** $8 + 6 =$ _____

**12.** $5 + 8 =$ _____   **13.** $6 + 3 =$ _____

**14.** $5 + 3 =$ _____   **15.** $8 + 4 =$ _____

**16.** $5 + 7 =$ _____   **17.** $4 + 7 =$ _____

**18.** $3 + 8 =$ _____   **19.** $4 + 8 =$ _____

**Partners, Teams, and Paper Clips**

# Pennies and Paper Clips (page 1 of 2)

Write an equation. Solve the problem.
Show your work.

**1.** Franco had 100 pennies. He used 67 of them to buy a baseball card. How many pennies does he have left?

**2.** There were 100 paper clips in the box. Kira pinched 52 of them. How many paper clips are left in the box?

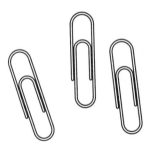

# Pennies and Paper Clips (page 2 of 2)

Write an equation. Solve the problem.
Show your work.

**3.** Sally had 100 pennies. She gave 26 of them to her brother. How many pennies does Sally have now?

**4.** There were 100 paper clips in the box. Jake pinched 19 of them. How many paper clips are left in the box?

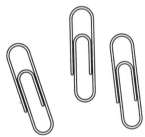

# How Many Stickers?

Write an equation. Solve the problem.
Show your work.

**NOTE** Students solve
a story problem.

SMH **70, 71–72**

**1.** Sally had 40 airplane stickers. She gave 27 of
them to Franco. How many airplane stickers does
Sally have now?

# Ongoing Review

**2.** There are 17 pennies in all.
How many are hidden?

(A) 14

(B) 13

(C) 11

(D) 6

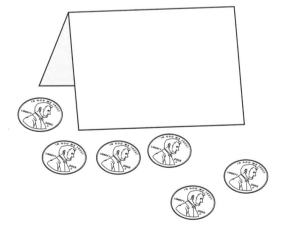

# Pinching Objects

Fill a cup with 100 small objects. You could use paper clips, toothpicks, beans, pennies, or buttons. For each round, pinch some of the objects to remove them from the cup. Count how many you pinched. Figure out how many are left.

**NOTE** Students practice subtracting amounts from 100.

**SMH** 73–75

Use the 100 chart if you need it.

**Round 1:**  I pinched _____. Equation: _____

There are _____ left in the cup.

Show how you figured out how many are left.

**Round 2:**  I pinched _____. Equation: _____

There are _____ left in the cup.

Show how you figured out how many are left.

# Story Problems (page 1 of 2)

Write an equation. Solve the problem.
Show your work.

**1.** Franco had 45 pennies on the table. He put 27 of them in his piggy bank. How many were still on the table?

**2.** Franco and Jake were playing *Cover Up* with 30 counters. Franco hid some of the counters. He left 16 showing. How many counters did Franco hide?

# Story Problems (page 2 of 2)

Write an equation. Solve the problem.
Show your work.

**3.** Sally had 41 rainbow stickers. She gave 16 of
them to Franco. How many rainbow stickers does
Sally have now?

**4.** There were 53 cherries in a bowl. Kira ate
17 of them. How many cherries were left?

# The Missing Fruit Mystery

Solve each problem. Show your work.

**NOTE** Students practice subtracting amounts from 100.

**SMH** 73–75

100 bananas          100 bananas

100 apples          100 apples

**1.** How many bananas are in the box? _____

How many bananas are missing? _____

**2.** How many apples are in the box? _____

How many apples are missing? _____

# Ongoing Review

**3.** Mom is 34, Dad is 35, Jake is 7, and Grandma is 58. Who is older than Mom and younger than Grandma?

(A) Mom          (B) Dad          (C) Jake          (D) Grandma

# More Story Problems (page 1 of 2)

Write an equation. Solve the problem.
Show your work.

**1.** Jake had 52 pennies. He spent 24 pennies on a new pencil. How many pennies does he have left?

**2.** Sally needs to climb 43 stairs to get to the top of the tower. She has climbed 28 stairs. How many more stairs does she need to climb to get to the top?

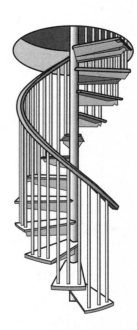

# More Story Problems (page 2 of 2)

Write an equation. Solve the problem.
Show your work.

**3.** Kira and Sally were playing *Cover Up* with
52 counters. Kira hid some of the counters.
She left 29 showing. How many counters did
Kira hide?

**4.** Franco had 55 marbles. He gave his brother
27 marbles. How many marbles does Franco
have now?

# Frog Stickers

Solve the problem. Show your work.

**NOTE** Students solve a story problem about groups of 10.

SMH **39**

**1.** Mr. Day has 113 frog stickers. He wants to give 10 frog stickers to each student. How many students will get 10 stickers? Are there any stickers left over?

# Ongoing Review

**2.** Kira has 1 quarter, 3 dimes, 2 nickels, and 6 pennies. How much money does she have?

(A) 56¢          (B) 66¢          (C) 71¢          (D) 81¢

# Paper Clip Problems (page 1 of 2)

**NOTE** Students solve related story problems about subtracting amounts from 100.

SMH 71–72, 73–75

Write an equation. Solve the problem.
Show your work.

1. There were 100 paper clips in a box. On his first turn, Jake pinched 13 paper clips. How many paper clips were still in the box?

2. Jake put all of the paper clips back into the box so that he had 100. On his second turn, he pinched 14 paper clips. How many paper clips were still in the box?

   How can you use the first problem to help you solve this problem?

# Paper Clip Problems (page 2 of 2)

Write an equation. Solve the problem.
Show your work.

**3.** There were 100 paper clips in a box. On her
first turn, Sally pinched 75 paper clips. How
many paper clips were still in the box?

**4.** Sally put all of the paper clips back into the box
so that she had 100. On her second turn, she
pinched 74 paper clips. How many paper clips
were still in the box?

How can you use the first problem to help you
solve this problem?

# Pennies and Stickers (page 1 of 2)

Write an equation. Solve the problem.
Show your work.

**1.** Jake had 72 pennies. He spent 58 on a new
pencil. How many pennies does he have left?

**2.** Kira had 86 sun stickers. She gave 53 of them
to her sister. How many sun stickers does Kira
have now?

# Pennies and Stickers (page 2 of 2)

Write a story that matches the problem.
Solve the problem. Show your work.

**3.** 65 − 38 = _____

_____

_____

_____

**4.**  62
      −45
      ‾‾‾

_____

_____

_____

# Picking Blueberries

Write an equation. Solve the problem.
Show your work.

**NOTE** Students use addition or subtraction to solve two story problems.

SMH 71–72, 78–80

**1.** Sally needs 100 blueberries to fill her basket.
She has picked 47 blueberries. How many more
does she need to pick to fill the basket?

**2.** Jake picked 54 blueberries. He used 38 of them
to make blueberry muffins. How many
blueberries does he have now?

## Ongoing Review

**3.** How many more students have a dog
than have a cat?

(A) 3      (C) 6

(B) 5      (D) 9

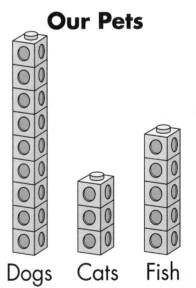

**Our Pets**

Dogs    Cats    Fish

# Stickers to Share

Write an equation. Solve the problem.
Show your work.

**NOTE** Students solve subtraction story problems.

**SMH** 71–72

**1.** Jake had 82 butterfly stickers. He gave 46 of them to Sally. How many butterfly stickers does he have left?

**2.** Sally had 71 basketball stickers. She gave 33 of them to Kira. How many basketball stickers does she have left?

# What Is the Fraction?

What fraction of the flag is gray? Black? White?
Write the fraction for each color.

**NOTE** Students use what they know about fractions to determine how much of a flag is shaded a certain color.

**SMH** 86, 87

**1.**

Gray: _____

**2.**

Gray: _____

Black: _____

White: _____

**3.**

Black: _____

White: _____

**4.**

Black: _____

White: _____

Gray: _____

**5.**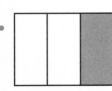

White: _____

Gray: _____

# Addition Problems, Set 1 (page 1 of 2)

Write an equation. Solve the problem.
Show your work.

**1.** Kira had 48 balloons. Jake gave her 33 more balloons. How many balloons does Kira have now?

**2.** Use a different strategy to solve this problem. Show your work.

# Addition Problems, Set 1 (page 2 of 2)

Write a story that matches the equation. Solve the
problem. Show your work.

**3.** 44 + 26 = _____

_____

_____

_____

_____

**4.** Use a different strategy to solve this problem.
Show your work.

# Addition Problems, Set 2 (page 1 of 2)

Write an equation. Solve the problem.
Show your work.

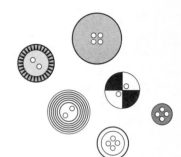

**1.** Franco had a collection of 57 buttons. He bought 34 more buttons. How many buttons does he have now?

**2.** Use a different strategy to solve this problem. Show your work.

# Addition Problems, Set 2 (page 2 of 2)

Write a story that matches the equation. Solve the problem. Show your work.

3.    14
    +49
    _____

_____

_____

_____

_____

4. Use a different strategy to solve this problem. Show your work.

Name Date



# What Time Is It?

Read each clock. Record what time it is and write the time in words. Then record and draw what time it will be in 2 hours and write the time in words.

**NOTE** Students practice telling, recording, and determining the time to the hour and the half hour.

SMH 139, 141

| What time is it now? | | What time will it be in 2 hours? | |
|---|---|---|---|
|  | 8:00<br>eight o'clock |  | : |
|  | : |  | : |
|  | : |  | : |
|  | : |  | : |
|  | 3:00 |  | : |

# Addition at Home (page 1 of 2)

Write an equation. Solve the problem.
Show your work.

**NOTE** As students solve two story problems, they write equations, add 2-digit numbers, and find different ways to solve a problem.

SMH 63–66

1. Jake had 39 pennies. His mother gave him 22 more pennies. How many pennies does he have now?

2. Use a different strategy to solve this problem. Show your work.

# Addition at Home (page 2 of 2)

Write an equation. Solve the problem.
Show your work.

**3.** Sally had 24 stamps. Jake gave her 67 more
stamps. How many stamps does she have now?

**4.** Use a different strategy to solve this problem.
Show your work.

# Addition Problems, Set 3 (page 1 of 2)

Write an equation. Try to solve the problem by keeping one number whole. Show your work.

**1.** Kira counted 49 ladybugs on the tree and 28 ladybugs on the ground. How many ladybugs did Kira count?

**2.** Franco had 66 car stickers. Jake gave him 52 car stickers. How many car stickers does Franco have now?

# Addition Problems, Set 3 (page 2 of 2)

Write a story that matches each problem.
Solve the problems. Show your work.

**3.**   55
       +36

_____

_____

_____

_____

**4.** 17 + 62 = _____

_____

_____

_____

_____

# Going to the Movies

**NOTE** As students solve two story problems, they write equations, add 2-digit numbers, and find different ways to solve a problem.

**SMH** 63–66

Write an equation. Try to solve the problem by keeping one number whole. Show your work.

**1.** On Monday, 38 people went to a scary movie. 56 people went to a funny movie. How many people went to the movies on Monday?

**2.** On Tuesday, 23 people went to a dinosaur movie. 49 people went to a shark movie. How many people went to the movies on Tuesday?

# Ongoing Review

**3.** Which combination does **not** make 100?

(A) 90 + 9     (B) 80 + 20     (C) 70 + 30     (D) 60 + 40

# Writing Stories (page 1 of 2)

Write a story that matches the problem.
Solve the problem. Show your work.

**NOTE** Students write stories that match the given problems and practice adding 2-digit numbers.

**SMH** 63–66

**1.** $37 + 48 =$ _____

_____

_____

_____

_____

**2.** Use a different strategy to solve this problem.
Show your work.

# Writing Stories (page 2 of 2) ✏️

Write a story that matches the problem. Solve the
problem. Show your work.

**3.**    63
       +29
       ———

_____

_____

_____

_____

**4.** Use a different strategy to solve this problem.
Show your work.

# Addition Problems, Set 4 (page 1 of 2)

Write a story that matches the problem. Try to
solve the problem by adding tens and ones.
Show your work.

**1.**    27
     +65
    ___

_____

_____

_____

_____

**2.** 42 + 53 = _____

_____

_____

_____

_____

# Addition Problems, Set 4 (page 2 of 2)

Write an equation. Try to solve each problem by keeping one number whole. Show your work.

**3.** Jake had 88 paper clips. He found 16 more paper clips in the hall. How many paper clips does Jake have now?

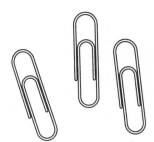

**4.** Sally had 73 marbles. Franco gave her 25 marbles. How many marbles does Sally have now?

# Today's Number: 12

Today's Number is <u>12</u>.

| |
|:---:|
| 42 – 30 |
| 50 – 20 – 10 – 8 |
| 12 – 0 |

**NOTE** Students write expressions that equal Today's Number by using only subtraction. There are many possible solutions.

SMH 55

**1.** Write at least five different ways to make Today's Number. Use only subtraction.

# Ongoing Review

**2.** What time will it be in three hours?

(A) 3:45    (C) 6:45

(B) 5:45    (D) 12:45

# More Addition at Home (page 1 of 2)

**NOTE** As students solve two story problems, they write equations, add 2-digit numbers, and find different ways to solve a problem.

SMH 63–66

Write an equation. Solve the problem. Show your work.

1. Sally had 48 skateboard stickers. Her brother gave her 36 more skateboard stickers. How many does she have now?

2. Use a different strategy to solve this problem. Show your work.

# More Addition at Home (page 2 of 2)

Write an equation. Solve the problem.
Show your work.

**3.** Franco had 63 truck stickers. Kira gave him 34 more. How many truck stickers does he have now?

**4.** Use a different strategy to solve this problem. Show your work.

**Partners, Teams, and Paper Clips**

# Addition Problems, Set 5 (page 1 of 2)

Write an equation. Solve the problem.
Show your work.

**1.** Kira had 69 beads. Jake gave her 19 more beads to make a necklace. How many beads does she have now?

**2.** Franco counted 46 pretzels in his bowl. Sally counted 58 pretzels in her bowl. How many pretzels do they have in all?

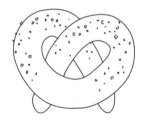

**Partners, Teams, and Paper Clips**

# Addition Problems, Set 5 (page 2 of 2)

Write a story that matches each problem.
Solve the problems. Show your work.

3.  41
    +74
    ‾‾‾‾

_____

_____

_____

_____

4. 64 + 35 = _____

_____

_____

_____

_____

# More Subtracting Tens

Solve these problems. Fill in
the totals on the 100 chart below.

 **NOTE** Students practice subtracting 10
and multiples of 10 from any number.

**SMH 24**

**1.** $83 - 10 - 10 - 20 =$ _____   **2.** $94 - 30 - 10 =$ _____

**3.** $85 - 40 - 10 - 20 =$ _____   **4.** $79 - 20 - 10 =$ _____

**5.** $91 - 50 - 10 - 10 =$ _____   **6.** $32 - 20 - 10 =$ _____

**7.** $67 - 10 - 10 - 30 =$ _____   **8.** $58 - 30 =$ _____

**9.** Fill in the other missing numbers on the 100 chart.

| | | | | | | | | | |
|---|---|---|---|---|---|---|---|---|---|
| 1 | | 3 | | | | 7 | | | |
| 11 | | | 14 | | | | | | 20 |
| | | | | 25 | 26 | | | | |
| | 32 | | | | 36 | | 38 | 39 | |
| 41 | | | 44 | | | 47 | | | |
| | 52 | | | 55 | | | 58 | | |
| 61 | | | 64 | 65 | | | 68 | | 70 |
| | | 73 | | | | 77 | | 79 | |
| 81 | 82 | | | | 86 | | | | 90 |
| | | | 94 | | | | | 99 | |

# Evens, Odds, and Combinations (page 1 of 2)

Solve each problem. Show your work.

**NOTE** Students review what they know about adding odd and even numbers and practice two of the remaining addition combinations.

SMH 41–42, 53

**1.** There are 13 girls and 11 boys in Ms. Wong's class. They are going to play a game in pairs. Will everyone have a partner?

**2.** There are 17 boys and 13 girls on the playground. They are going to play a game of soccer. Can they make two equal teams?

# Evens, Odds, and Combinations (page 2 of 2)

Solve each problem. Show your work.

**3.** Kira has trouble with 7 + 9. Write a clue
that will help Kira remember 7 + 9.

$$9 + 7 =$$

$$7 + 9 =$$

Clue: _____

**4.** Franco has trouble with 8 + 6. Write a clue
that will help Franco remember 8 + 6.

$$6 + 8 =$$

$$8 + 6 =$$

Clue: _____

# Prize Tickets (page 1 of 2)

At the spring fair, Robin wins
200 prize tickets.

**NOTE** Students solve real-world problems involving the math content of this unit.

**1.** Which prizes could she get
with 100 tickets?

| | | | |
|---|---|---|---|
| 🚗 | Car: 20 tickets | Bear: 20 tickets | 🧸 |
| 🧢 | Hat: 45 tickets | Ball: 20 tickets | ⚽ |
| 🐸 | Frog: 10 tickets | Eraser: 5 tickets | |

Show your work. Write an equation.

# Prize Tickets (page 2 of 2)

**2.** Which of these prizes could Robin get with the other 100 tickets?

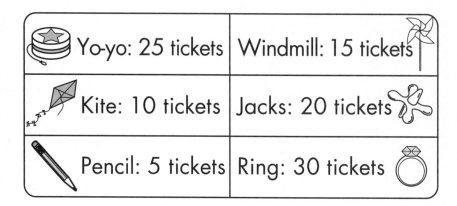

| | |
|---|---|
| Yo-yo: 25 tickets | Windmill: 15 tickets |
| Kite: 10 tickets | Jacks: 20 tickets |
| Pencil: 5 tickets | Ring: 30 tickets |

Show your work. Write an equation.